MAP READING

by

Robert B. Matkin

Illustrations by R. Martyn Jones

DALESMAN

DALESMAN PUBLISHING COMPANY LTD.
CLAPHAM, via Lancaster, LA2 8EB

First published 1979
Second edition 1984
Third edition 1992

© Robert B. Matkin 1979, 1984, 1992

ISBN: 1 85668 042 4

Front Cover: Extract from Ordnance Survey Map Landranger 98,
Wensleydale and Upper Wharfedale. Scale 1:50,000
© Crown copyright

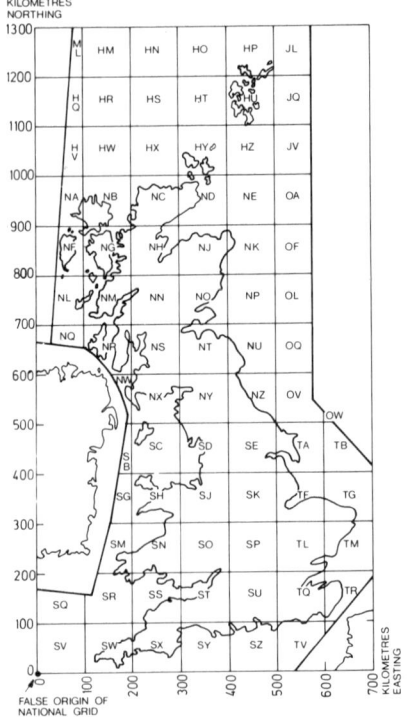

Printed by Peter Fretwell & Sons Limited,
Goulbourne Street, Keighley, West Yorkshire BD21 1PZ

Introduction

THE motorist who speeds along the road misses a great deal of the countryside that flashes past his window. The hiker, walker or rambler on the other hand does not travel nearly so fast or go so far, but he sees very much more — like the wild flowers, the birds and those little footpaths that meander down from the main road and disappear into the woods or follow the banks of a river, by the waterfalls, and up along the dales and over the bracken covered fells and moors.

Motorist and walker have one thing in common in that they can both lose their way, or ar least they could if they did not have a map. But a map is not much good unless you have the right one, can understand its language and know how to read and use it to find your way or plan your route. This booklet aims to help by discribing techniques that are essentially practical, simplifying rather than confusing the art of map reading. If it succeeds, it can only add to the enjoyment of 'being about' in the countryside.

National Parks

Some areas of the open countryside are specially protected against development which would destroy the character of the landscape; they are called National Parks. They have been designated for public enjoyment and include areas of moorland, mountains and woodland. The public have no special rights in these Parks; most of the land is still privately owned and some Parks include whole towns and villages. The largest of the National Parks are the Lake District, Snowdonia, Yorkshire Dales and the North York Moors.

Nature Reserves and Trails

There are dozens of Nature Reserves and Trails throughout the country specially devoted to informing the visitor about wild life and plants of the area. The National Park's Information Service will be able to give information where they are to be found within the Parks.

(See also Cautionary Notes, page 32)

1 Ordnance Survey

THERE is a wide range of maps published by the O.S. with scales from 1:250 to 1:1 000 000. A scale of say 1:25 000 indicates that one unit on the map represents 25 000 units on the ground (in plan). For example, 1cm on the map represents 250 metres on the ground.

A large scale map shows a small area with a lot of detail and is not much good for long journeys, whilst a small scale map will show a large area with much less detail and would be of little use to the walker or cyclist. No one scale of map suits everybody's needs.

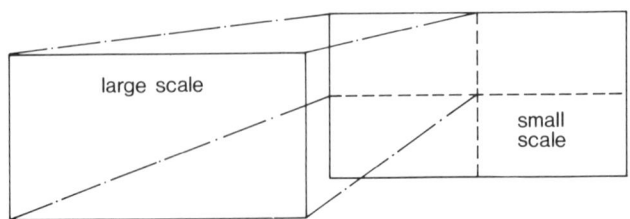

Area of one sheet 1:25 000 scale.   Area of one sheet 1:50 000 scale. (The dotted lines indicate the area of a 1:25 000 map.)

The three most suitable scales for use by walkers are the 1:50 000, the 1 inch to 1 mile and the 1:25 000. The 1 inch to 1 mile maps have largely been replaced by the 1:50 000.

The 1:25 000 scale maps will show the best footpaths to follow and which way is likely to be the easiest. All the sheets of the three scales mentioned show marginal data (Section 2), the National Grid (Section 4) and contour lines (Section 5).

The 'in plan' (see above) is mentioned because the distance A–B might be up a steep hill and would be longer than that measured in the plan.

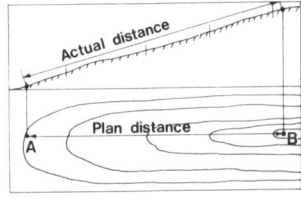

Special Maps

These have been produced to cover areas of interest to tourists and hikers. In the 1 inch 1 mile series there are nine editions which

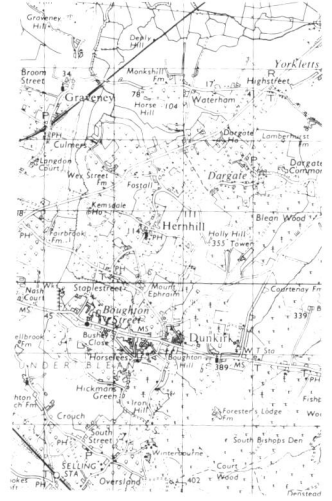
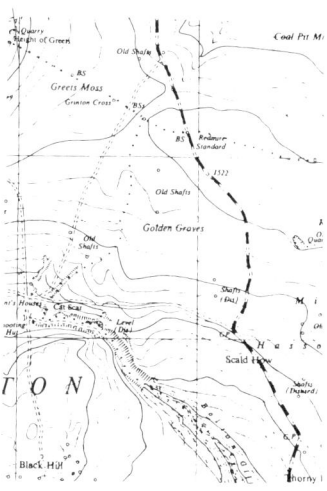

One inch to one mile (1:63 360)   1:25 000

include the Peak District, Lake District and North York Moors.
At a scale of 1:25 000, there are a growing number of Leisure Maps and these include the English Lakes, Malham and Upper Wharfedale, the Three Peaks of Whernside, Ingleborough and Pen-y-Ghent and the Dark Peak (Derbyshire Peak District). Each of these maps covers an area of about 500 sq. kilometres and contains certain information and hints for travellers. They show tourist features such as caves, waterfalls and view-points.

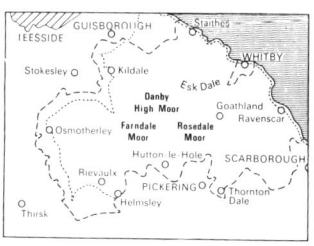

Long Distance Paths

There are over a dozen long distance paths in Great Britain, several of which are now open throughout their entire length. The 1:50 000 scale sheets covering some of the most popular are numbered:
    Pennine Way — 74 80 86 91 92 103 109 110.
    Cleveland Way — 93 94 99 100 101.
    Pembrokeshire Coast Path — 145 157 158.
    Offas Dyke Path — 116 117 126 137 148 161 162.
    South Downs Way — 197 198 199.

Further information on Ordnance Survey maps can be obtained from your local O.S. agent or map stockist.

2 Marginal Data

IT is essential to study the information contained in the margins — the area of paper surrounding the map — for it shows a lot of detail that is essential to the use and understanding of the map. The styles of presentation of this marginal data will vary from one map scale or series to another, but as a general rule the information is almost the same. Considering a 1:50 000 First Series map, the marginal data is:

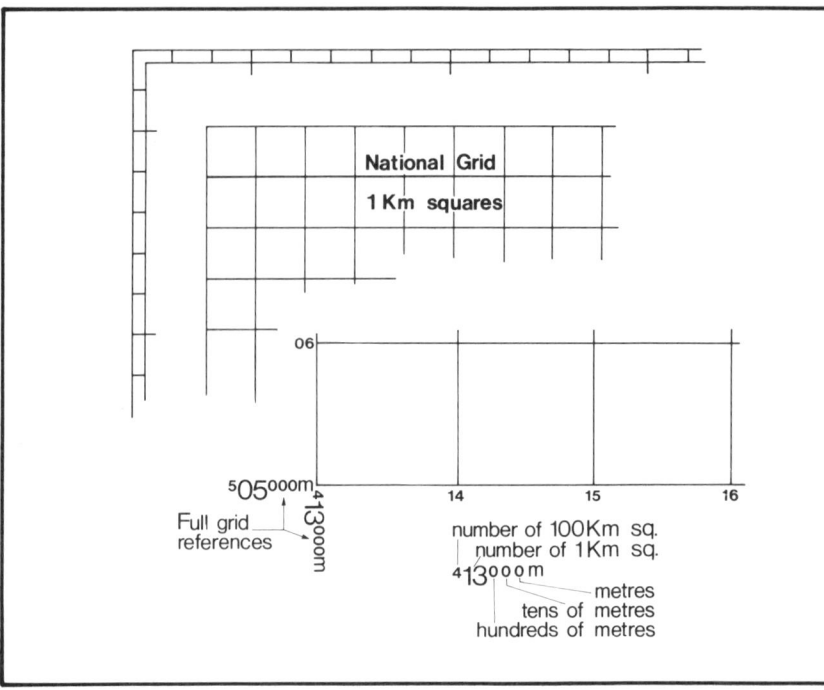

Information on latitude is printed in the outer borders of the sheet. Full degrees are shown in heavy type where they occur. Near each corner is shown the degrees and minutes; other values are shown in minutes only at every 5 minute interval (see next page). The small crosses (+) that appear over the whole map are the intersection points of the 5 minute intervals of latitude and longitude.

Some Signs and Symbols

Wood mixed	⚲⚵⚲⚵	Marsh	ᵂᵂ ― ᵂᵂ	Quarry	
Bracken, Heath & Rough Grassland			Minor Road Drive or Track	═══════════ ─ ─ ─ ─ ─ ─ ─ ─ ─ ─	
Cliffs	⌂⌂⌂⌂	Footbridge	─┤├─	Youth Hostel	▲ red
Church & Spire	+ ●	Church & Steeple	+ ■	Triangulation Pillar	▲ blue
Public Right of Way	Footpath Right of way on foot Bridleway Horses or walking Road used as public footpath			─ ─ ─ ─ ─ ─ ─ ─ ─ ─ ─ ─ ─ ─ ─ ─ ⊥ᴛ⊥ᴛ⊥ᴛ⊥ᴛ⊥ᴛ⊥	

TITLE
SHEET NUMBER
SCALE

List of how features are indicated on the map — roads, public rights of way, railways, water, general features (symbols and conventional signs).

Relief — how contours are shown, their values and contour interval.

Boundaries.

Abbreviations e.g. P=Post Office, T=Telephone Call Box.

Antiquities.

Scale (see Section 12).

Grid Reference (see Section 3).

North Points (see Section 5).

Compilation and revision dates.

Index to 1:50 000 series — map showing sheet numbers over Great Britain.

The vertical lines (Eastings) of the National Grid are numbered along the top and bottom margins from left to right, and the horizontal lines (Northings) along the side margins from bottom to top. A full grid reference of the lines is given at the corners.

3 National Grid

O.S. MAPS have superimposed upon them a series of vertical and horizontal lines called the National Grid. The whole country is covered by the grid which has its origin or starting point south-west of the Scilly Isles. The squares are lettered (see inside front cover). As the lines in both directions are numbered and carried forward from sheet to sheet, the grid provides an easy means of locating detail just by giving a number — known as a Grid Reference. The largest squares have sides of 500km and these are each divided into 25 squares of 100km side.

According to the scale of the map, these 100km squares are subdivided into smaller squares. For the three scales we are considering, these smaller squares have 1km sides. NORTH is to the top of the maps and one set of lines runs North to South (Eastings) and the others East to West (Northings).

To give a Grid Reference

1. Determine the grid letters of the 100km square (found in the marginal data of the map). In this case it is SE.

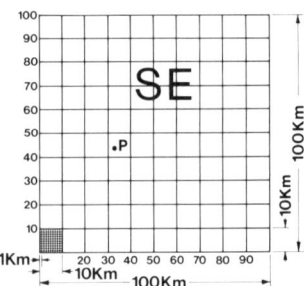

2. The 10km square in which point P lies is located by the numbers of the grid lines which form the bottom left-hand corner. There will be two numbers, one for the vertical and one for the horizontal lines. These numbers must always be given in the right sequence. The first number refers to the vertical line forming the West edge — as the square lies to the East of this line it is called an Easting. The next number is the horizontal line forming the South edge of the square — the square lies to the North of this line and is called a Northing. Eastings first, Northings second. In the example

the two numbers are 3 and 4 and the Grid Reference is therefore SE34. No mark or space is put between the numbers, and there must always be the same number of figures for an Easting and Northing.

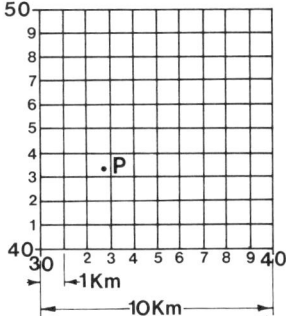

To define the position of P more precisely, the 10km square is divided into squares of 1km side. Point P can now be defined by adding two more Grid References for it lies in the 1km square 2 East and 3 North, Grid Reference is now SE3243.

As the 1km squares are shown on the O.S. map we are using, a closer grid reference could be given if they in turn were sub-divided into 10 vertical and horizontal lines, locating P in one of the new squares. This can be done by estimating the number of tenths or using a ROMER. This is a piece of card or plastic, the top and right-hand side having distances of 1km drawn to the scale of the map and sub-divided into tenths. Place the top right corner (zero mark)

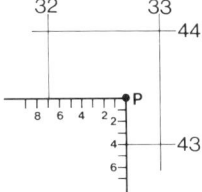

against the point and the edges parallel to the grid lines. The distance of the point from the grid line can be read off directly for both Easting and Northing. In this case 7 and 4. Adding these to the reference already found, it becomes SE 327434 and is called a six figure Grid Reference, locating a point to 100m on the scales being considered. The letters may be omitted (give sheet number instead), even though a reference is repeated every 100km square.

4 Contours

THE shape of a fell or dale is quite easily seen when viewed in relation to the surrounding country, i.e. the sides of a fell are steep or gently rising, or some part is much higher than the rest, and such information is very important to a walker. As a map gives only a bird's-eye view on a flat sheet of paper, some means must be used to show these changes in ground level. This is done by using what are called contour lines.

A contour line is an imaginary line joining points on the ground which are the same height above a datum or zero level which has been established by the O.S. at Newlyn, a fishing village in Cornwall. On the O.S. maps, these contours are shown by a light brown line (1" to 1 mile) or an orange line (1:50 000 and 1:25 000).

The shape of the contours indicates the shape of the ground. When they are far apart the slope of the ground changes slowly. When they are close together the ground level changes rapidly. Contour lines are continuous however far they run, the only exception being at a vertical cliff face where the contours merge. The contours are drawn at regular vertical intervals, i.e. the difference in height between successive lines. This interval varies according to the scale of the map:

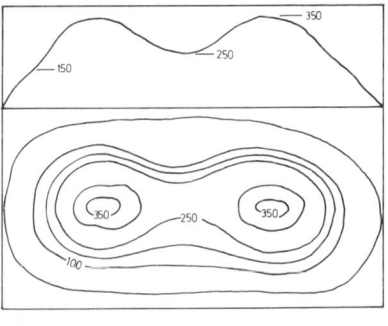

    1:25 000 — vertical interval is 25 feet.
    1:50 000 — vertical interval is 50 feet with the contour values
                   given to the nearest metre.
    1"–1 miles — vertical interval is 50 feet.

The contour values are shown in breaks made in the contour lines and are placed so that they read the right way up when looking up the slope. To help in reading, some of the contour lines are thickened at regular intervals:

    every 100 feet on 1:25 000 scale.
    every 200 feet on 1"–1 mile scale.
    every 70 metres on 1:50 000 scale, this corresponding to the
    nearest metric conversion of 250 feet.

Some forms of contour lines are:

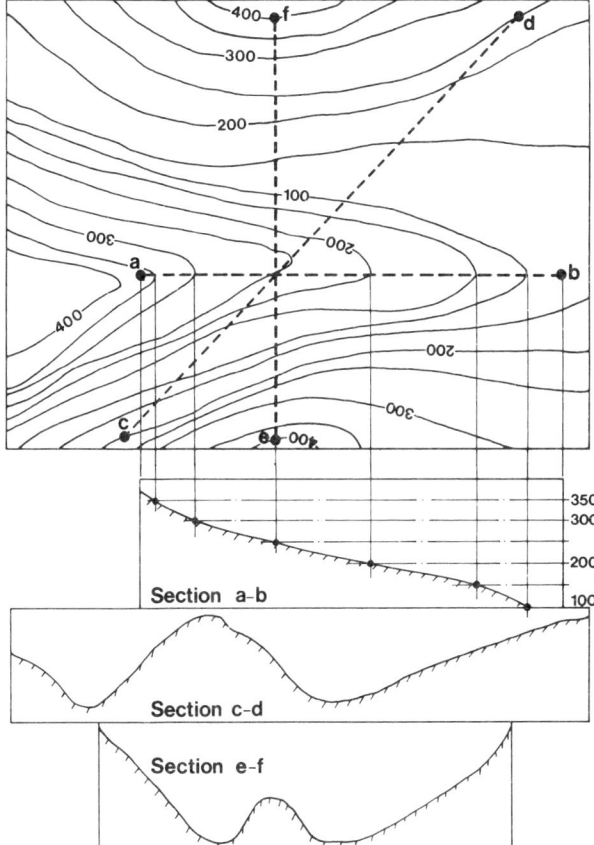

The shape of the ground at the various sections can be found as described in Section 11. In addition to contour lines, local high points on the ground (called spot heights) are shown. They are indicated as a black spot with the height in feet/metres printed alongside.

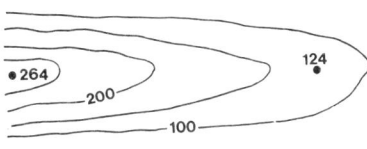

5 Types of North

THERE are three types of NORTH used in mapwork:

TRUE — the actual direction of the North Pole, one end of the axis on which the Earth rotates.

MAGNETIC — the direction towards which one end of the compass needle points.

GRID — the direction of the vertical grid lines from the bottom to the top of the map.

The only two NORTHS which concern the map reader are Grid and Magnetic. It is sometimes useful to know how to find True North and, whilst the O.S. map gives the relative position of the three Norths in the marginal data, together with information regarding magnetic variation, there are some simple ways it can be found (see Section 14).

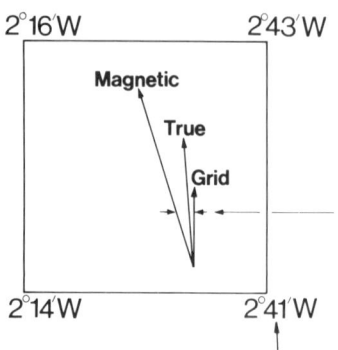

MAGNETIC NORTH
In 1979, Magnetic North is about 9° West of Grid North, decreasing about ½° every eight years.

TRUE NORTH
The difference between True North and Grid North is given at the corners of the sheet.

The reason for the variation between True and Grid North at different points of the map is because of the difficulty in representing the curved surface of the Earth on a flat sheet of paper. The relative directions of True and Grid North vary for different maps. West of a line through the Bournemouth area, True North lies to the East of Grid North.

6 The Compass

THE magnetic north pole lies to the west of True North, and is situated in the Upper Hudson Bay area of Canada. Its position varies slightly year by year; the variation is stated on Ordnance Survey maps (see Section 5). From our knowledge of magnets, we know that the magnetic south end of a compass needle always points to magnetic north. As the compass will be used for determining the angle between a line and magnetic north, the housing surrounding the needle is divided into 360 divisions called degrees.

The type of compass most often in use by the map reader, and also the one used to illustrate map work in this book, is the SILVA compass. This one is the Mark 4 version. It is basically the same as an ordinary compass but with some additional features to assist map reading.

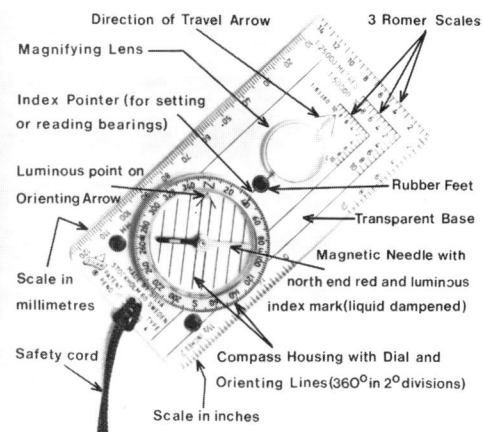

To take a Magnetic Bearing with a Compass

1. Hold the compass horizontal at about waist height so that the direction of travel arrow points to the feature.
2. Keeping the base of the compass steady in this position, turn the housing until the North on the rim is opposite the red end of the needle.
3. Read off the number of degrees at the index pointer. This is the Magnetic Bearing.

Compass needles are attracted magnetically to nearby metal objects. Avoid taking readings where any 'local attraction' could affect the true magnetic reading.

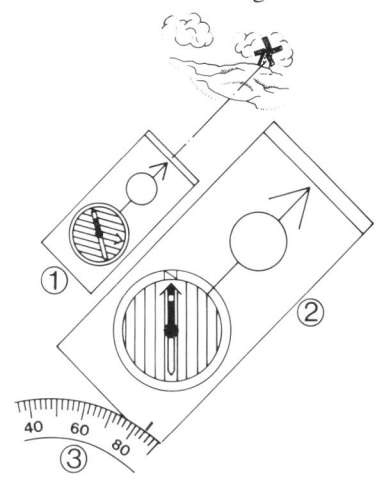

7 Bearings

WHEN walking in the open country or at the most along a footpath, it will be necessary at some time to check the position one is at or determine the direction along which to continue travelling. Using a map and compass together, this is done by taking bearings, either from the ground or from the map. A bearing is the horizontal angle observed between any point and North. As has been seen in Section 5 there are three types of North, so it follows there are three types of bearings.

A TRUE BEARING is the angle between a point and True North. Here point A is on a True Bearing of 78°.

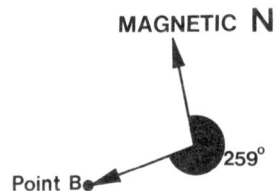

A MAGNETIC BEARING is the angle between a point and Magnetic North. Here point B is on a Magnetic Bearing of 259°.

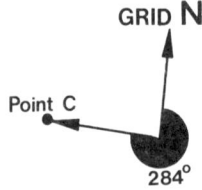

Similarly, a GRID BEARING is the angle between the point and Grid North. Point C is on a Grid Bearing of 284°.

Note that bearings are always measured in a clockwise direction from the North, and, as there are 360 degrees (360°) in a circle, a bearing can be of any number of degrees from 0 to 360.

Map readers rarely use the True North because the O.S. maps generally in use will have grid lines giving the direction of Grid North, and the compass will give a bearing relative to Magnetic North. As has been seen there is a variation between Grid and Magnetic North and it is necessary to allow for this variation when bearings are taken by compass and transferred to the map and vice-versa. If Magnetic North is taken as being 9°W of Grid North the necessary correction to be made are:

(Ground to Map)

Magnetic Bearing of point L (observed over the ground by compass)	=	86°
Subtract variation 9°W	=	−9°
Grid Bearing of point L (plotted on the map using a SILVA compass)	=	77°

Magnetic Bearing to Grid Bearing

Grid Bearing to Magnetic Bearing

(Map to ground)

Grid Bearing of point M (observed on map by a SILVA compass)	=	204°
Add variation 9°W	=	+9°
Magnetic Bearing of point M (used to indicate a direction)	=	213°

NOTE

A simple technique that does away with all the bother of remembering whether to add or subtract the variation of 9° is to stick a small strip of paper on the bottom of the capsule of the SILVA compass, marking on it the exact position of 351° (the 9°W variation). In both cases (Magnetic to Grid or Grid to Magnetic) the compass needle is pointed at the 351° mark and not at the North point.

SILVA compasses can be bought at most sports shops.

15

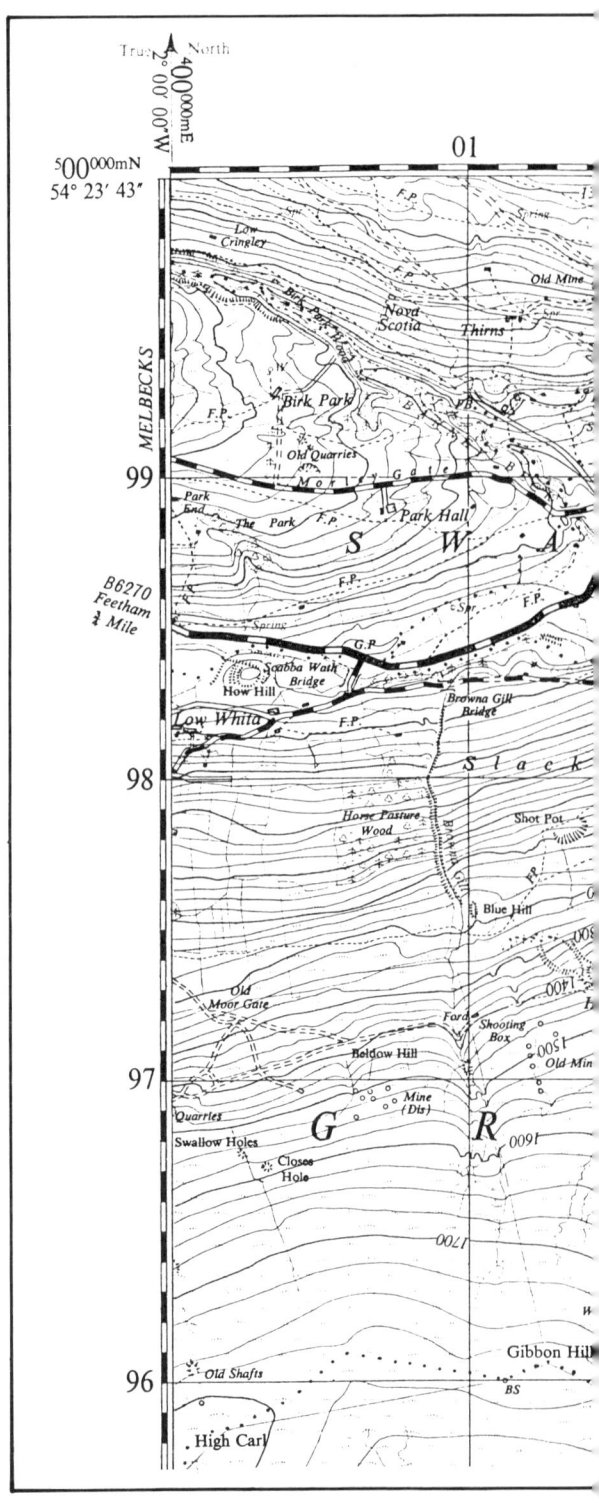

Extract from 1:25 000 (First Series) Ordnance Survey map, sheet SE 09, showing the area around Reeth in Swaledale, North Yorkshire.

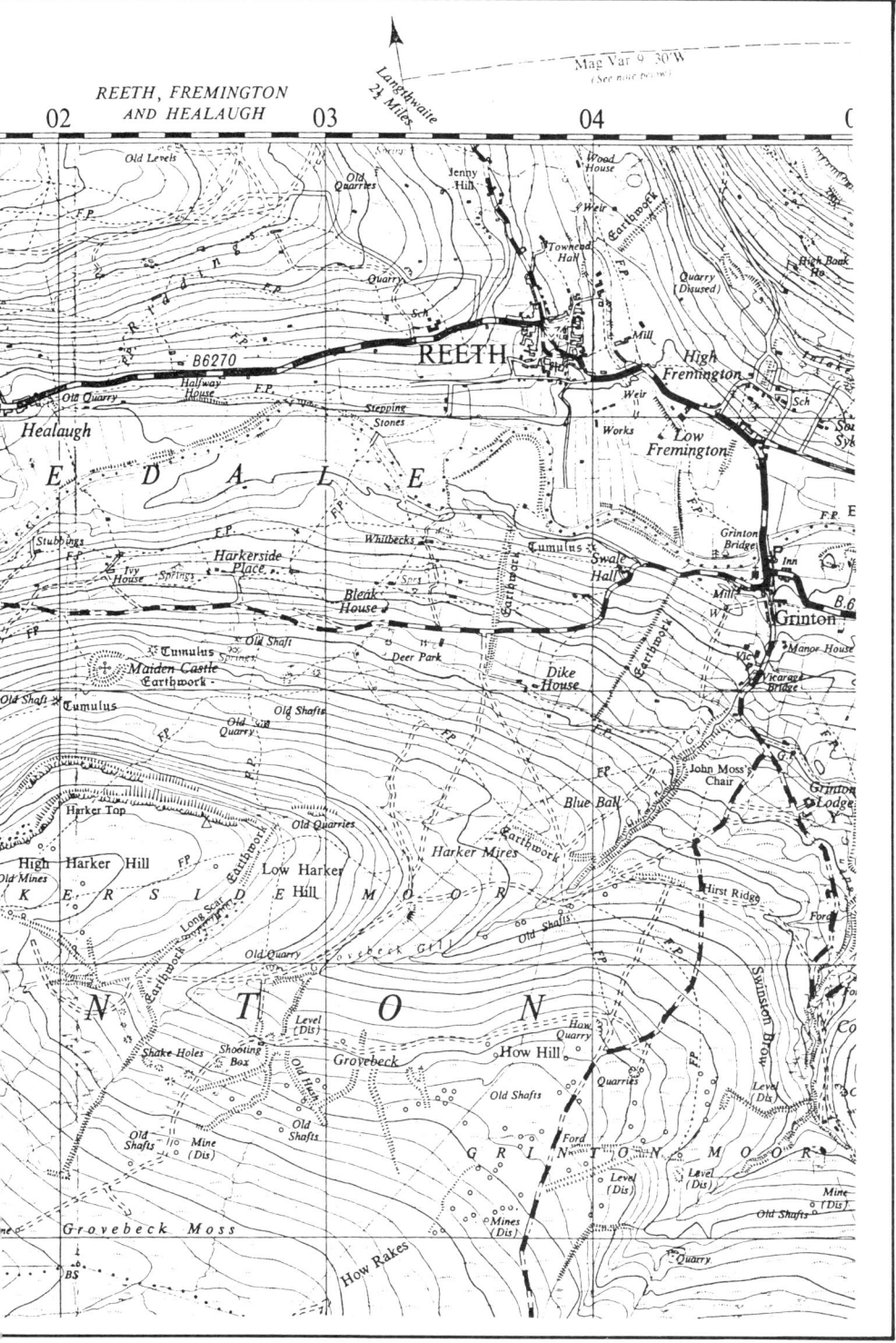

8 Where am I?

TO find the position where you are at any time can be done by the method of 'resection' or cross bearings. Two points are chosen on the landscape and their positions identified on the Ordnance Survey map. They should preferably be at an angle of about 90°; a small angle gives a poor intersection.

Double bearing

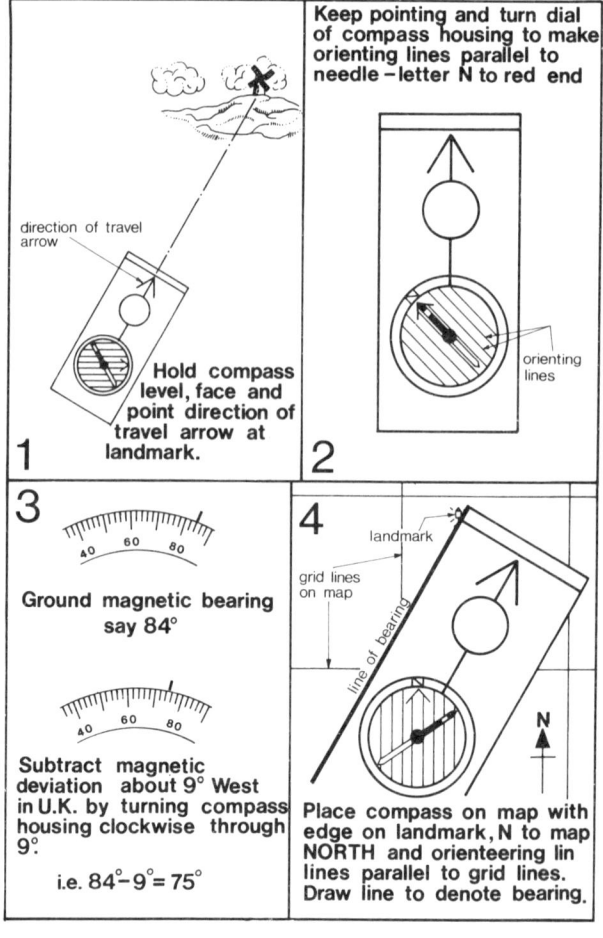

Repeat the same procedure on the second point, taking a magnetic bearing, reduce to a grid bearing, orientate on the map and draw the second line. Where the two lines intersect will be your position.

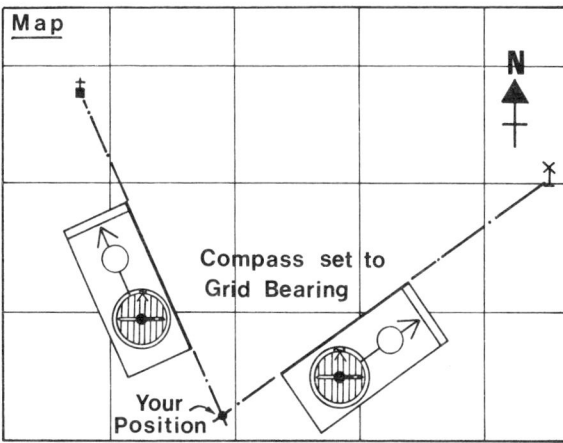

Greater accuracy can be obtained by selecting a third point and then drawing another bearing line. It is possible that the lines will not meet exactly but should form a small triangle. Your position will generally be within the triangle.

Single bearing

If your position is known approximately, as when for example walking along the ridge of a hill, then only one magnetic bearing need be taken, converted to a grid bearing and plotted. Your position will be where this line cuts the ridge you are on.

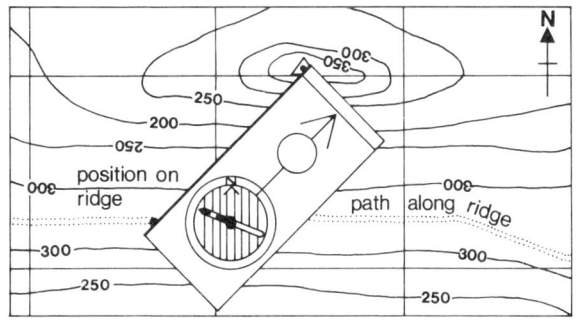

9 Which way to go (1)

THERE are three ways in which the direction it is required to travel can be transferred from a known position on the O.S. map to the actual ground.

1. **By Orientating or Setting the Map**

Hold the map so that the top faces the direction of North (see Section 12 for finding the direction of North without a compass), and the printing is right way up.

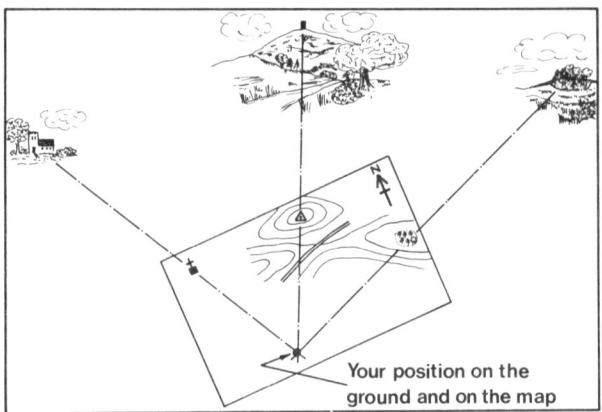

A map is set or orientated when the position of features on the ground corresponds with the same features on the map. Select a feature on the ground and find its position on the map. Turn the map round until an imaginary line through your known position and the map feature chosen intersect the same feature on the ground. Keeping the map steady (it is best to lay it flat on the ground), select another feature and by the same process adjust the map slightly so that your imaginary line again intersects your position on the map and the ground feature. The map is now orientated.

It is only a matter of following the direction of the line of a chosen route on the map and continuing it out on to the landscape to see the line of travel (see Section 10 — Walking a bearing).

2. Orientating the Map with a Compass

The compass is first set with the index pointer opposite the number of degrees of magnetic variation to Grid North. With the map on a flat surface, place the compass on it so that the direction of travel arrow lies along a vertical grid line and pointing to the North edge of the map. Gently turn the map with the compass on it until the red arrow of the compass needle points to the North on the rim of the compass housing. The map is now orientated. The direction of the chosen route can now be followed as before — or the compass itself can be used to determine the direction of travel.

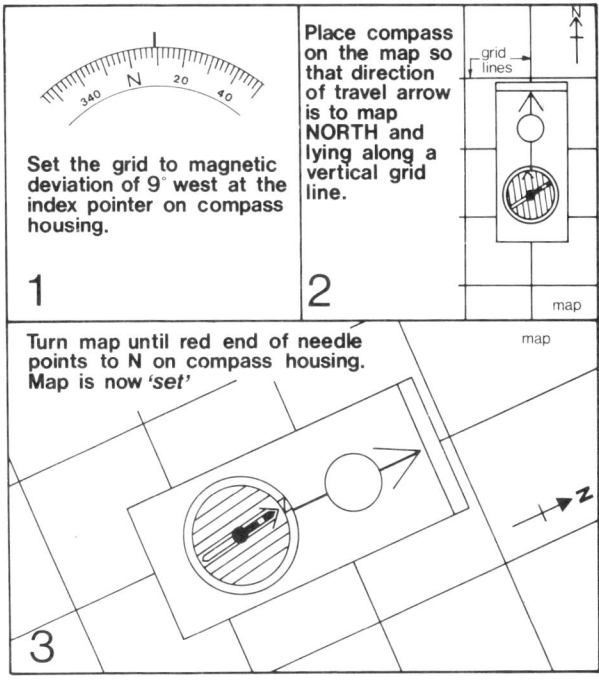

10 Which way to go (2)

3. Compass Bearing from Map to Ground

Taking a bearing from a map and facing the same bearing on the ground is the reverse procedure of ground to map bearings.

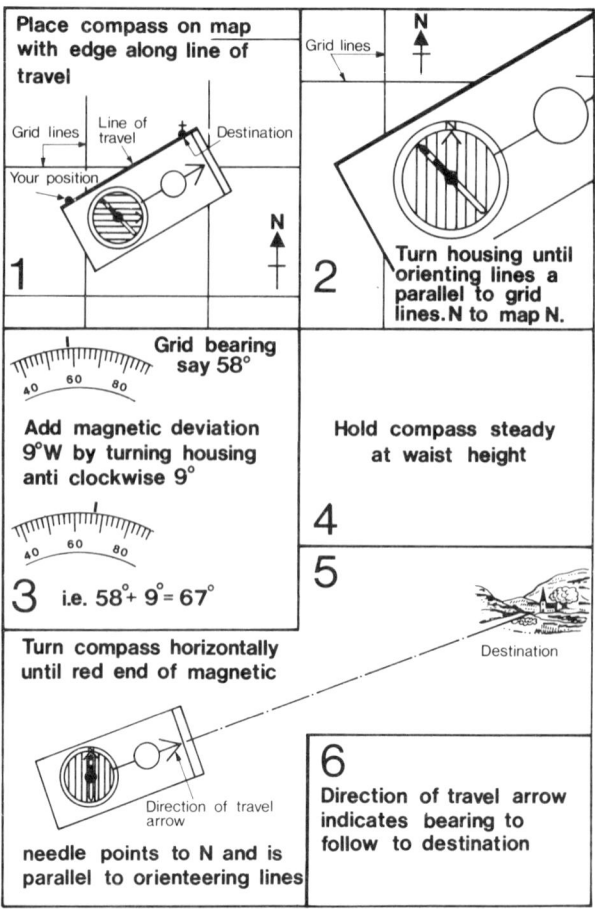

Having set the compass to the required bearing from the map it can now be used to face and walk the bearing as follows.

Facing a Bearing

Face, approximately, the chosen direction. Hold the compass in the hand at waist height and level enough to allow the needle to swing freely, the direction of travel arrow pointing ahead. Hold the compass steady and turn your body until the red end of the compass needle points to the North mark on the housing. The required bearing is now shown by the direction of travel arrow.

To Walk a Bearing

Having faced the required bearing, look ahead and choose a landmark or point on the ground in line with the direction of travel arrow on the compass. Walk to the chosen spot and repeat the process until the destination is reached.

A check can always be made that the right direction has been followed to a point by taking what is called a back bearing. After arriving at the point, turn and face the direction that has been travelled. Holding the compass as before and without altering the dial setting, line up the red end of the needle opposite the South mark on the compass. The direction of travel arrow should now point to the spot from which the original bearing was taken.

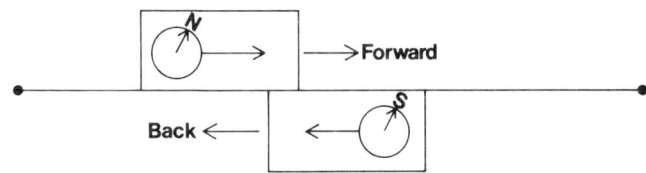

NOTE

Accuracy in using the compass, both in setting and walking a bearing is important and it is worth taking a little extra time over the exercise. A hurried calculation or a rough alignment of the compass could lead to some trouble, particularly if the journey is over difficult or dangerous ground.

11 How steep is it?

THE steepness of a hill — normally defined as the gradient — can be very important to anyone walking, for it can be very tiring and time consuming on a long journey.

Gradients are expressed in one unit rise in so many units length.

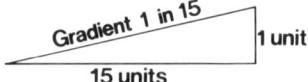

By studying the contours on an O.S. map, the gradient for any portion of a journey can be calculated. In addition, maps indicate steep gradients on roads thus:

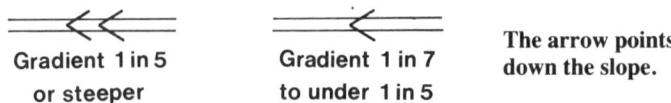

Gradient 1 in 5 or steeper

Gradient 1 in 7 to under 1 in 5

The arrow points down the slope.

The gradient of any portion of a line drawn on a map can be determined by measuring the horizontal distance between successive contours and expressing this in the same units as the contour interval.

Gradient between A-B:
30m in 120m or 1 in 4.

Gradient between B-C:
30m in 150m or 1 in 5.

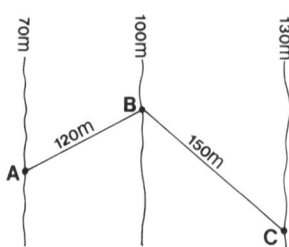

Naturally the steepest gradient on a route occurs where two succesive contours are closest together.

It is difficult to visualise gradients on a map, and it is better to draw them to scale from measurements taken off the map itself as follows. A portion of country with contour lines only is shown indicating a proposed route:

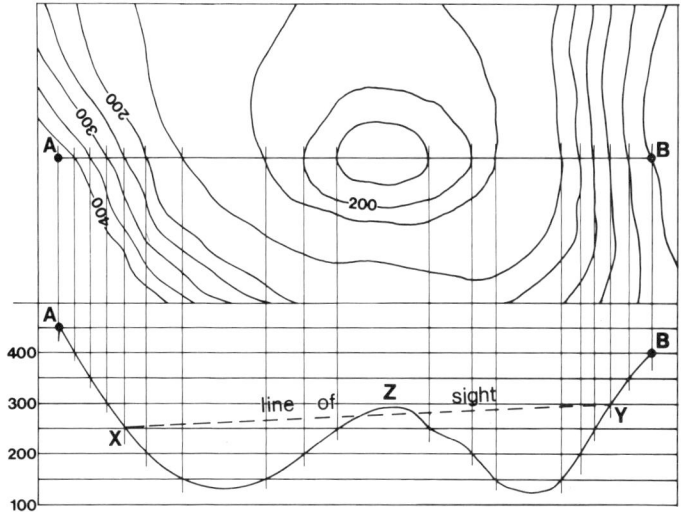

On one edge of a piece of paper draw a grid of a series of equally spaced horizontal lines representing the successive contours. From the points on the map where the route crosses a contour, draw vertical lines down to the grid, marking the appropriate horizontal line corresponding to the contour height. A line joining these points will indicate the steepness. It is not always convenient to use the same scale for the vertical contour line spacings on the grid as that used for the map scale, for this might be the result:

This would not indicate anything about gradients. Instead, make the contour vertical lines on the grid to a distorted scale of say 3mm for each 5m contour line on a 1:50 000 map.

Intervisibility. The same system can be used to find if any point is visible from another. In the route shown above, it can be seen that a straight line from X–Y (a line of sight) cuts the high ground at Z. It would not be possible therefore to see the ground at Y from the ground at X. A further point that might have to be considered is the height of trees or other obstacles on the sight line.

12 How far is it?

ALL maps are drawn to a scale and this scale is shown in the map margin. There are several ways to determine the distance between two or more points using this drawn scale. If the shortest distance between two points is needed it is only necessary to place the edge of a piece of paper between the points on the map and mark off their distance on the paper.

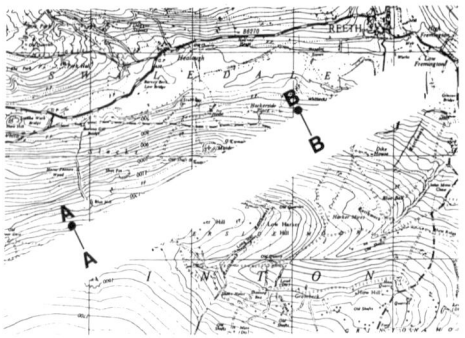

The paper is then placed against the drawn scale and the distance read off. A ruler or some dividers could have been used to determine the distance between the points, afterwards transferring the distance to the map scale as before.

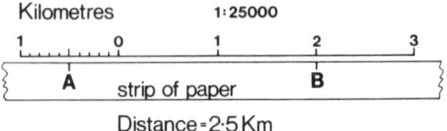

The grid lines, being 1km apart, can be used to give a quick approximation of distance.

Roads and footpaths are not usually so straight and to get an accurate measurement of distance it is necessary to take into account bends and corners. A rule in this case is not much help but the paper method is. Using the straight edge of the paper, put a pencil mark at one end and place this mark at the starting point on the map.

Consider the route to be measured as being a series of short straight lines. Put another mark at the end of the first straight, or nearly straight section. Turn the paper so that the edge lies along the next straight section with the second mark on map and paper

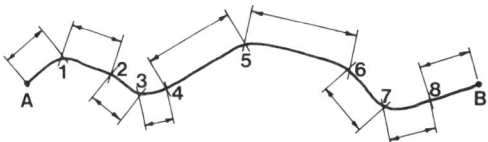

together. Mark off the end of the second section. Repeat until the end of the route is reached. The edge of the paper will now be marked like this:

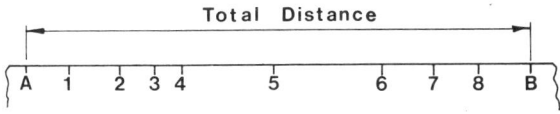

As before, place the paper against the drawn scale on the map and read off the total distance. String could be used instead of paper, making a mark on it corresponding to the start and finish. If there are any hills along the line, the horizontal distance must be adjusted to take into account the slopes.

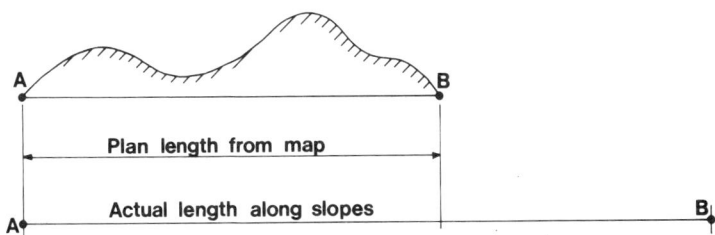

A pair of dividers or compasses could be used to step off a distance, counting the number of steps to cover the whole route — the steps should be short. By repeating the same number of steps against the drawn map scale, the distance can be found.

An instrument called an opisometer or map measurer can be used. Here a small wheel traces out the route to be taken, the distance the wheel travels being shown directly on a scaled marked on a dial.

Miles per hour

As a guide, a walker travelling at a reasonable speed covers about 2–2½ miles per hour. A runner going at a slow trot covers about 6–7 miles in the hour, but these distances depend on the individual. It is useful to know how far one can travel for route planning purposes (Section 13) and this is best found by experiment over a measured distance.

13 Selecting routes

THE preceding sections have shown how to read and use a map, and how to recognise what the ground will look like from the information given. The map signs and symbols, the identification of ground features and a knowledge of the steepness of the ground from the contours are all points to be understood. Map reading is an art that needs practice. Unless the chosen route is to be along well defined footpaths or roads, a decision will have to be made about a choice of route. For example:

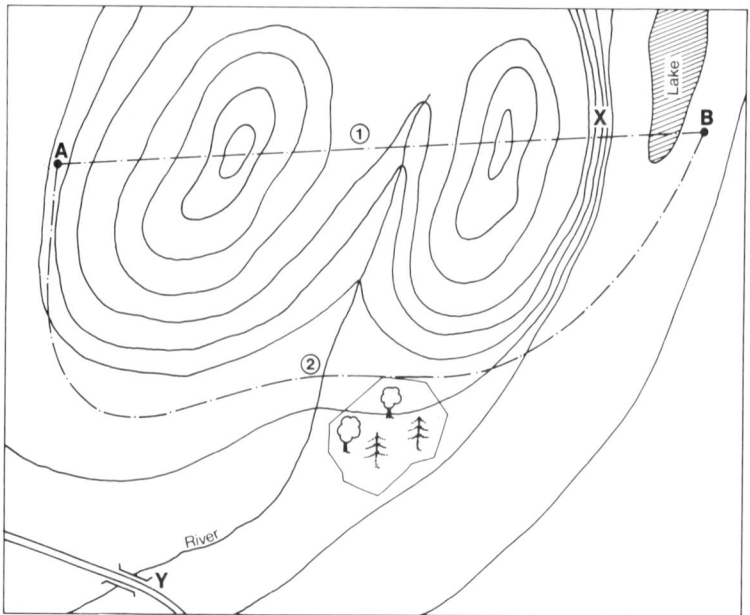

Route (1) is the shortest in distance but requires climbing up two hills, crossing a stream and negotiating a steep cliff at point 'X'. There is also a lake which will have to be avoided.

Route (2) is nearly twice as long but it nearly follows the line of the contours (known as walking the contours); this indicates there is very little climbing to do. It passes through a wood but touches only along the edge. There is a river to cross which, if it is in full flood (perhaps after heavy rain), might mean a small diversion to cross over by the road bridge at 'Y'.

As an exercise look at the map in the centre fold and decide a route to be followed between the two grid references 040963 and 004993, making the distance as short as possible (note the River Swale).

In selecting a route, it is a good idea to first draw a straight line between the start and finish and see if this route can be taken. If not, then try and select one that follows as close to the theoretical one as possible. Points which should be considered when planning a route are:
1. Obstacles — cliffs, water (river or lake), fences, mines and private property.
2. Nature of the ground — hills, valleys, escarpments, marshes and thick woods.
3. Would a longer journey but using paths be better?
4. Are there special features that can be used as landmarks, churches and buildings, fence lines or stone walls which are a guide over difficult land?
5. Intervisibility between the landmarks chosen.
6. The more contour lines that are crossed, the more climbing or descending that has to be done.

Strip Maps

Shown here are portions of two strip maps. They can be drawn, not to scale, after a route has been planned on the O.S. map. Such a map will be useful on the journey in addition to the scale map for it can be used to show details of ground features, road numbers and any other information that it is thought necessary.

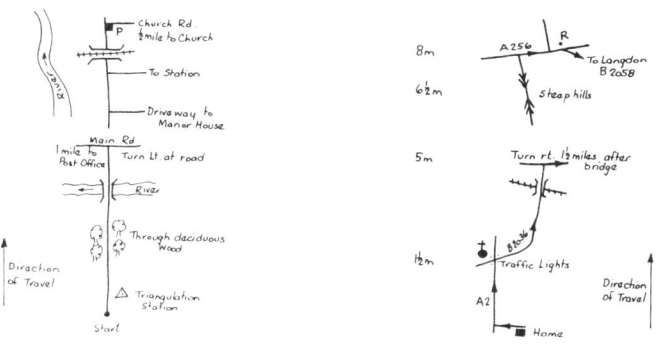

For the Walker **For the Cyclist**

NOTE: To keep maps dry in wet weather, put them into a clear polythene bag, they can still be quite easily read.

14 General information

IN Section 5, mention is made of True North. Whilst a compass should always be carried, it might get lost or broken and some means of determining direction would have to be used. This could be done if the direction of True North were known. It can be found in two easy ways, by the sun during the day (that is if it is shining) and by the stars at night (if cloudless).

By the Sun and Watch

The figures and diagrams opposite are given for British Summer Time. For Greenwich Mean Time, one hour should be deducted.

The sun reaches the highest point in the sky at 13.00 hours, when it is due South. By holding a watch pointing the 1 on the dial towards the sun (due South) the position of 7 gives the direction of True North, 4 the West and 10 the East. One point — make sure your watch shows the correct time before starting on a journey. (Fig. A).

It is not always convenient to wait for the sun to be in the due South position, and the way to find True North at any hour the sun is shining is as follows. By holding the watch flat in the palm of the hand, point the hour hand towards the sun (ignore the minute hand). Due South will be in the direction of a line drawn through the centre of the watch and midway between the hour hand and 13.00 hours (Fig. B).

By night

A map can be orientated at night by lining the True North sign on it with the Pole Star. The Pole Star is found in the constellation Great Bear, sometimes called the Plough. By following the stars round, two of them can be seen to point to a third — the Pole Star. (Fig. C).

To orientate a Map with a Watch

Place the watch on the map and line the sun with the hour hand. Keeping the watch still, turn the map until the South end of the North–South line points in a direction midway between the hour hand and 13.00 hours. The map is then orientated North and South. (Fig. D).

Fig. A

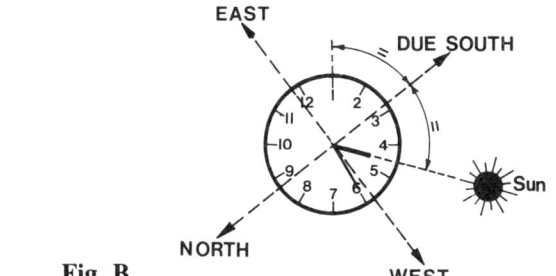

Fig. B

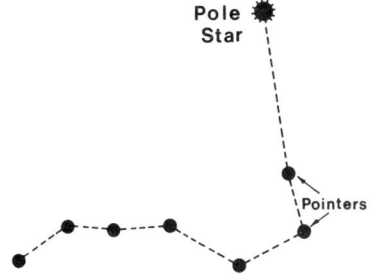

Fig. C

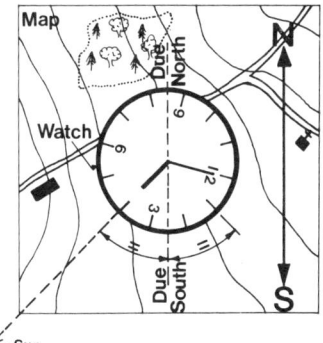

Fig. D.

15 Cautionary Notes

THE weather can change dramatically over high ground in a very short time, so be prepared by carrying waterproof clothing. A polythene sheet and some boiled sweets are useful in case you get 'holed up' somewhere away from civilisation, especially in winter time. Always carry a compass and Ordnance Survey maps of the area you are in. Should bad weather descend quickly, make sure you have plotted your position on the map before the landscape disappears in the mist. A whistle is useful as it can be blown to guide anyone to your position should you have had an accident.

When planning a route from your O.S. map, pay special attention to features which might be dangerous or cause problems to your progress. We have already seen in Section 2 how some of these features are shown; others will be found in the marginal data of the map in use.

Woods and forests are very easy to get into, but not so easy to find your way out. This is where a map and compass are invaluable. Cross fast flowing rivers by a footbridge, especially after heavy rain when they fill with water very quickly. Keep clear of open pits, mines, caves and fissures in rocks.

Always tell someone the route you are prosposing to travel, particularly if it is over some of the wilder parts of moor or fell and, if possible, some indication of the time you expect to be back or reach your destination. By doing this, you could perhaps save a lot of time and worry to others.

★ ★ ★ ★

The portion of a 1:25 000 (First Series) Ordnance Survey map, sheet SE09, in the centre fold and other map examples in the text are Crown Copyright Reserved and reproduced with the sanction of the Controller of H.M. Stationery Office. The published sheets are in full colour.

Acknowledgements
SILVA COMPASSES (London) LTD.
THE WILDLIFE YOUTH SERVICE